# OSCARS

# CONTENTS

**Endpapers: Photo by Dr. Herbert R. Axelrod.**

ISBN 0-87666-765-5

© 1982 by TFH Publications, Inc. Ltd.

Distributed in the U.S. by T.F.H. Publications, Inc., 211 West Sylvania
Avenue, PO Box 427, Neptune, NJ 07753; in England by T.F.H. (Gt. Britain)
Ltd., 13 Nutley Lane, Reigate, Surrey; in Canada to the pet trade by Rolf C.
Hagen Ltd., 3225 Sartelon Street, Montreal 382, Quebec; in Canada to the
book trade by H & L Pet Supplies, Inc., 27 Kingston Crescent, Kitchener,
Ontario N28 2T6; in Southeast Asia by Y.W. Ong, 9 Lorong 36 Geylang,
Singapore 14; in Australia and the South Pacific by Pet Imports Pty. Ltd.,
P.O. Box 149, Brookvale 2100, N.S.W. Australia; in South Africa by Valid
Agencies, P.O. Box 51901, Randburg 2125 South Africa. Published by T.F.H.
Publications, Inc., Ltd., the British Crown Colony of Hong Kong.

# oscars

by neal pronek

# INTRODUCTION

The purpose of this book is to tell people who don't know very much about oscars enough to enable them to keep the fish in good health over a long period of time. Oscars are very enjoyable to own if their owners meet them halfway and make real efforts to provide the fish with the kind of maintenance they need. They can become true pets if their demands for space and care are met, but if they are not given what they need they will be pests instead of pets. Therefore the information in this book is given partly by way of instruction, mostly for those neophyte oscar owners who feel that they could use some guidance in the care of their fish, and partly by way of warning, mostly for those who don't own oscars but would like to know what owning one entails if it is to receive the treatment it should have.

The oscar shown below is a juvenile, about 1½ inches long. This is the ideal size at which oscars should be purchased. As juveniles, oscars are much more adaptable to a new environment than they are as adults. The photo on the opposite page is of a red oscar, a color strain developed by commercial breeders. Photos by Dr. Herbert R. Axelrod.

# *1.*

# OSCARS IN GENERAL

## POPULAR NAMES

The fish most commonly known to American aquarium hobbyists as the oscar is also known to them as the peacock cichlid, and velvet cichlid. The names peacock cichlid and velvet cichlid are more common in Great Britain and other present and former members of the British Commonwealth than they are in the United States, but all three names (and a few others, too) have achieved a degree of currency in all English-speaking lands that harbor aquarists.

The name peacock cichlid is descriptive of the fish in that the oscar is indeed a cichlid, and adult oscars indeed bear at least one marking in common with a peacock: the dark spot, surrounded by a circle of lighter color, near the base of the oscar's tail is similar to the "eye spot" on a peacock's tail. The velvet cichlid name, probably derived from the comparative smallness of the scales, also is descriptive, but to a much lesser degree; the velvety look of an adult oscar, although present if you're inclined to look for such things, is much less evident than the eye spot. The name oscar is neither descriptive nor strictly apropos in any other way . . . but it has stuck. I don't believe that anyone knows for sure how a fish like this one had the name "oscar" tagged onto it, but the name has been around in the aquarium hobby almost as long as the fish itself, and that's more than forty years.

Probably "oscar" is derived from a name an early importer of the species placed on it for reasons of his own or is a corruption of its scientific name or some local South American native name for it.

## SCIENTIFIC NAME OF THE OSCAR

Originally named *Lobotes ocellatus* by Baron Cuvier in the early 1800's, the oscar is now known to science as *Astronotus ocellatus,* a name that seems unlikely to change. *Astronotus* means being marked with a star on the back, and *ocellatus* means bearing an ocellated marking, or "eye spot." Many other fishes have a reference to an ocellated marking of one type or another incorporated into their scientific names, so the oscar is by no means unique in this regard. Another fish so described is *Cichla ocellaris,* whose ocellus is even more noticeable, although smaller. If you want to get into a big hassle about the function of the oscar's ocellus, go ahead. Reams have been written about the function of such markings on fishes, but no acceptable conclusion has been drawn, nor is it even demonstrable that such markings have any function at all.

## THE OSCAR'S FAMILY

*Astronotus ocellatus* belongs to the family Cichlidae, a group of almost completely freshwater fishes found mainly in the Americas and Africa, with a small representation in Asia. No one knows how many cichlids there are, because new species are being discovered all the time, and the geographical range of both African and American cichlids is far from exhaustively explored for new piscine fauna.

Cichlids differ widely in size, body shape, coloration, temperament and breeding habits. Such popular fishes as the peaceful little ram (*Apistogramma ramirezi*) and

The photo above shows a tributary of the Amazon River, near Tefe, Brazil. It was in this general locality that Dr. Herbert R. Axelrod found oscars having a highly variable pattern of ocelli along the base of the dorsal and caudal fins (below and opposite, lower photo). Photos by Dr. Herbert R. Axelrod.

Oscars bred in captivity generally seem to have only one ocellus, which is most often centrally situated at the base of the tail. Contrast this to the ocelli on the wild-caught oscar shown below. Photos by Dr. Herbert R. Axelrod.

the nervously graceful angelfish (*Pterophyllum scalare*) as well as the colorful but highly aggressive jewel fish (*Hemichromis bimaculatus*) and big, temperamental oscar are all cichlids.

## INTELLIGENCE IN THE OSCAR

Apart from the morphological differences that have set cichlids apart from other fishes, they all share in varying degrees in one trait that has made them, as a group, more popular than they otherwise would be: they're smarter than most other aquarium fishes. By this I mean that they're comparatively smarter; they show a greater degree of purposiveness in their actions than most other popular aquarium fishes do. They seem to be a good deal more aware of what's going on around them, a trait usually lumped under the catchall statement that they have "personality." If you would compare, for example, the actions of a group of angelfish or oscars or Egyptian mouthbrooders as they live out their lives in a big aquarium with those of a group of zebra danios or tiger barbs or neon tetras in an equally large tank, you'll know exactly what "personality" means in a fish. The seemingly mindless, frenetic pacing of the barbs and danios and tetras contrasts vividly with the actions of the cichlids, who move more slowly but with more determination from place to place in the tank. Other fishes dash; cichlids explore.

It's that way with oscars. They seem to know what they're doing. Although cichlids may not be the most intelligent of all aquarium fishes (they are outranked in one usual important measure of the relative intelligence of animals, the comparison of brain weight to total body weight, by the fishes of the family Mormyridae, the elephantnoses of Africa, for example), they're right up near the top, and the oscar is one of the smartest of the cichlids.

Oscars may not always *look* very smart, but don't sell them short. Photo by Gunter Senfft.

A head-on view of a domesticated red oscar. Notice the protruding eyes of this fish. Novice hobbyists, upon noticing the eyes beginning to bulge as their oscars mature, sometimes begin to treat their fish with an assortment of medications. Bulging eyes are normal for mature or maturing oscars and should not be treated with any kind of medication unless the eyeballs actually protrude from their fleshy sheaths. Photo by Dr. Herbert R. Axelrod.

Because of their large size and predatory nature, oscars should be kept only in the company of other large fishes that are capable of self-defense. The fish shown behind the oscar is a *Cichlasoma managuense.* It also is a large predatory cichlid, and in a large enough tank it will live quite peaceably with an oscar. Photo by Dr. Robert Goldstein.

It may look dopey, but this African elephant-nose (family Mormyridae) is smarter than an oscar if you use the yardstick of brain weight to total body weight as a comparison point. Photo by Klaus Paysan.

This last statement is the result of observation and discussion with other hobbyists, not of laboratory tests. Few tests have been made to determine the relative intelligence of the various cichlid species, but judging by my own experiences and those of others in the hobby, oscars are among the most savvy of all cichlids. They are not alone in their capacity to be trained to perform simple tricks like ringing a bell to obtain food, but they seem to take to teaching more readily, and with a greater enjoyment, than other species. They have a greater degree of awareness of their keepers than most other fishes, and they are one of the very few piscine species that seem even remotely able to respond to human affection in any way.

In this regard, oscars reign supreme in the freshwater aquarium world. They and certain other large cichlids are the closest things to true pets—as opposed to just interesting subjects of observation—that the freshwater aquarium hobby produces. (I make the qualification about freshwater fishes here because certain saltwater species, among the groupers and batfishes most notably, rival or surpass oscars in the capacity to respond to human beings.)

And oscars can make fine pets. They have been known to seek out friendly hands placed into their tanks, languorously brushing themselves against the hands much in the same way that a dog approaches to be petted, and it has often been claimed that they can differentiate between their owners and other people. Behavior like that is decidely un-fishlike, and it has helped to make the oscar one of the perennially most sought after of aquarium species.

## POPULARITY OF THE OSCAR

Oscars have personality, and from the standpoint of maintaining their popularity, it's a good thing they do, because they don't have much else going for them. They're not especially colorful or graceful, they're too big for most hobbyists' tanks, they're bullies, they're fairly tough to feed, they're messy eaters and even greater messer-uppers of tank arrangements . . . so why are they consistently sought after by hobbyists who know them and their ways?

I think it's because they're more interesting than most other fishes, and they're more interesting because they behave more humanly than other fishes. Watch an oscar rearrange gravel and rockwork in his tank to suit himself, resisting your most determined efforts to put things

The Texas cichlid, *Cichlasoma cyanoguttatum* (opposite), is the only cichlid that is native to North American waters. It is found in the Rio Grande basin. It can reach a length of about 12 inches, and at that size it makes a good tankmate for a large oscar. Photo by Hans Joachim Richter. *Cichlasoma citrinellum* (above), like its very close relative the red devil, *C. labiatum,* is a highly predatory species, but in a large aquarium it will generally get along quite well with an oscar. Photo by Klaus Paysan.

Adult oscars of the size shown here (an adult *Cichlasoma* shown under the fish at left for purposes of size comparison) would be guaranteed to attract plenty of attention in any well-appointed aquarium. Photo by Paul Zanolini.

where *you* want them, and you've watched an example of near-human stubborness . . . and the very willfulness of it is interesting. Watch oscars actively fight or threaten over possession of something and you've seen a display of bullyrag and braggadoccio that would be the envy of any human troublemaker . . . and it's interesting. Watch an oscar hunt down and engulf a food fish and you've seen real animal dominance in action . . . and it's interesting. Other fishes, cichlids especially, perform the same actions in one way or another, but they don't elicit as much attention as the oscar while they're performing them. Probably size has a lot to do with it.

Mature oscars are big fish by aquarium standards, and it's tough not to catch their act, whereas the actions of smaller species often go unnoticed. Ounce for ounce of body weight, for example, *Nanochromis nudiceps* will move a lot more gravel than an oscar, but *Nanochromis* at its largest is but a fraction of a mature oscar's size and therefore may go unwatched, whereas the actions of an oscar are unmistakable and bound to attract attention.

Regardless of the reasons for it, oscars definitely are popular. Adult oscars make good show fish in dealers' tanks and usually are among the highest-priced fishes in any given aquarium store. In early 1981, for example, the price of a good full-size oscar of the most common color variety (the regular oscar, not one of the newer color varieties) was $25 in a Brooklyn, New York aquarium specialty shop whose prices are fairly representative of the New York market. So the price of the same fish in the rest of the country probably would run to anywhere between $30 and $60. Baby oscars were $1.25 each and three-inch juveniles $3.50 each; they also would probably cost more outside the New York area. Full-size oscars may not be the most expensive fish in a shop, but they're right up near the top in price. And one big difference between high-priced oscars and high-priced oddballs like big snakeheads and *Colossoma* and other "show" fishes is that the oscars sell; if they're half-way decent, the dealer usually will be able to move them quickly, whereas he might have to give tank space to some of his other high-priced fishes for a long time.

That pretty much sums up the charm of the oscar as far as its popularity among aquarium hobbyists is concerned. It's a big, smart, interesting fish that happens also to be one of the money fishes of the hobby . . . that is, a species that is worth keeping and hopefully profiting from by breeding and raising the babies to sell. This last point is important in determining the popularity of

A mature oscar photographed at the exact moment it has begun to flare its branchiostegal membranes in an attempt to show its displeasure over something going on within its view. When oscars are displeased, they let you know it.

**Opposite:**
*Colossoma oculus* is a large characoid that will usually not battle with oscars housed in the same tank. Photos by A. Roth.

This baby oscar was 1¼ inches long at the time this photo was taken and shows much of the pattern of markings of the typical young regular oscar. Photo by Dan Sonye.

a species. Aquarium hobbyists are, despite the impression one might gain in print and in electronic media, normal human beings with a normal craving for making money out of the things they like to do for pleasure, and it's entirely natural for them to keep in the back of their minds the idea of turning an eventual nickel or two when choosing fishes for their tanks. Many a baby oscar has been sold on the basis of the notion in its purchaser's mind of its growing up to be a money machine when it reached spawning size. Many an adult oscar, or group of adult oscars, has been the object of considerable investment in money and tank space on the premise that it would soon pay for itself. These happy dreams of profit are almost always shattered in the end, because most oscar owners don't have the art or persistence necessary for them to capitalize on their investments . . . but as long as there is a good profit potential for the successful breeder and raiser of oscars, hobbyists will be interested in and willing to pay for adult *Astronotus.*

## AGGRESSIVE BEHAVIOR IN OSCARS

One important aspect of the oscar's behavior pattern has to do with the fish's deportment towards other fishes that inhabit the same tank. Although it has often been said that the oscar is mean or even vicious, I think that it is not, at least not in comparison to other fishes that unquestionably really merit such description. Oscars are not the most even-tempered of fishes, and they definitely have a tendency to bully tankmates of smaller size, but they are not out-and-out vicious. They will eat a fish that is small enough to be eaten, and they will lord it over smaller tankmates, cooping them up in corners of the tank and preventing them from coming out to get their share of the food, but they don't go around with the single-minded purpose of destroying every other fish they come into contact with, the way some other species do.

If they get their own way with other fishes they'll usually let matters rest at that point, not pursuing things to the point of outright killing. Truly mean-tempered, belligerent oscars are found, but not very often. An exception to this general rule of behavior for oscars is the temperament of the fish under spawning conditions. Mis-mated pairs sometimes fight to the death, with the bigger fish almost always being the killer. And oddly enough, aggressiveness in oscars decreases as the fish grow older and bigger; juvenile oscars are more belligerent than mature fish.

Oscars can be maintained in tanks housing other fishes, provided the other fishes are too big to be eaten or effectively bullied. Suitable tankmates in a "com-

*Uaru amphiacanthoides,* commonly known simply as the uaru, is a large, slow-moving fish with a surprisingly peaceful temperament for a cichlid. This species, however, can take care of itself quite well in the presence of other predatory fishes such as the oscar, so it can be kept quite successfully together with one or more oscars. Photos by Hiroshi Azuma.

Full-grown *Metynnis* and other "silver dollar" fishes make good tankmates for large oscars; unfortunately, they won't thrive on the items offered to oscars as food. Photo by Kremser.

These fully mature oscars were maintained in a very large tank in a public aquarium in Germany, where they were kept only with species of comparable size. Photo by Gerhard Budich.

munity" aquarium would include large catfishes and cichlids of a size comparable to the oscar's; big barbs like full-size tinfoil barbs also will get along with oscars, and so will big charaocid types such as *Anostomus* and *Leporinus* and *Metynnis*. But in general it's best to keep oscars by themselves.

## COLOR VARIETIES

Until just a few years ago there was only one color scheme to adult oscars: the regular kind, examples of which are shown in this book. Early in 1969, though,

At this small size (about one inch) baby oscars still tend to school. As the fish mature, the schooling tendency seems to disappear altogether, but as subadults oscars tend to form monogamous pairs. Together, the pair takes up the defense of its chosen territory, and this can occur long before the first spawning. Because of their rapid growth and potential requirement for a large territory, even baby oscars should be housed in a fairly large aquarium. Photo by R. Zukal.

Baby uarus also tend to school and follow a pattern similar to that of oscars in pairing off and staking out a territory. Baby uarus even look quite similar to baby oscars. The two species can be raised together in the same aquarium and will most likely get along well throughout their lives if they are not crowded. Photo by Hiroshi Azuma.

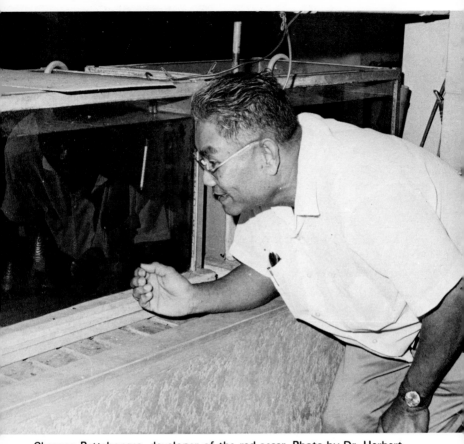

Charoen Pattabongse, developer of the red oscar. Photo by Dr. Herbert R. Axelrod.

the aquarium trade started to receive regular shipments of a fish known as the red oscar. The red oscar was a good-looking fish; in the opinion of many, it was better looking than the regular oscar, and it soon caught on in a big way. Today red oscars are available throughout the hobby, and it looks as if they'll stay popular. They were developed by a Thai businessman, Charoen Pattabongse, who discovered a few aberrant individuals in a group of regular oscars and developed his find into a true strain. Red oscars breed true and should be given the same care as normally colored fish. Another color variety of *Astronotus,* mid-way between the red oscar and the regular oscar in coloration, is the more recently developed tiger oscar, also called tiger red oscar and tiger stripe oscar. In my opinion, this variety isn't attractive at all and shouldn't be perpetuated, since it is no improvement on either the regular oscar or the red oscar, but there appears to be a market for them.

## DIFFERENCES IN APPEARANCE CAUSED BY AGE

Something entirely different from the consideration of color variation between strains of oscars is the consideration of the difference in appearance between baby oscars and juvenile oscars and between juvenile oscars and adult oscars. Baby oscars are patterned very differently from juveniles and adults. They are a deep brown, almost black, in over-all color, with an irregular network of creamy streaks all over the body. As the babies grow, the streaks gradually disappear and are replaced by the basic brownish-red adult coloration. Juvenile oscars are less colorful than adults and lack the ocellus, but they couldn't be mistaken for anything but oscars, whereas babies often are thought to be a different species altogether.

The least expensive baby oscars purchasable at pet shops are young fish and look very much like these wild-caught babies. These are regular (non-red) oscars; baby red oscars would not have the same marbled pattern. Photo by Harald Schultz.

As Oscars progress in age they grow quickly and lose the marbled pattern of the infant fish; these young oscars are considerably older than the babies shown above, but they are far from fully adult. The ocellus, for example, has not yet formed. Photo by Milan Chvojka.

This is a fully adult oscar showing the typical adult pattern of markings, including the ocellus; note also the extension of the ventral fins. Photo by Klaus Paysan.

## WHERE THE OSCAR COMES FROM

The normal range of wild *Astronotus ocellatus* is northern South America. The abnormal range of wild *Astronotus ocellatus* is southern Florida. Oscars are now established in waterways in Florida, where they are fished for as a sport and food fish; they are rated highly by fishermen for their fighting qualities, less highly for their taste. Oscars probably became established in Florida waters when some escaped from fish hatcheries situated in the state; they are not the only non-native species that have become established that way. Regardless of how they got there, they're probably there to stay. If you want to go to Florida and catch your own oscars on hook and line, try any kind of live bait or lure that a largemouth bass would take. If you file the barb off the hook you'll have a good chance of landing any oscar you come up against without hurting it severely.

## SIZE AND LONGEVITY

We've already mentioned that mature oscars are big fish by aquarium standards, but exactly how big do they get? Two separate questions are involved here, one being a consideration of the maximum size of an oscar maintained in captivity and one being the question of the maximum size reached by a fish in the wild. Generally wild fishes reach a much greater size than their counterparts that live most or all of their lives under aquarium conditions, so although somewhere there might be a wild 18-inch *Astronotus* patriarch living it up in unmolested majesty, you can consider that a tank-raised oscar that has reached a length of a foot is a truly large-size specimen, and any oscar bigger than that is a jumbo. If you give an oscar enough room to grow and the proper water and feeding conditions, there is no reason that, barring accidents, it shouldn't live for at least ten years, because oscars have been known to live under aquarium conditions for more than fifteen years.

# 2.

# HOUSING FOR OSCARS

## TANKS

In general, a big fish needs a big tank, and the oscar is no exception. As a matter of fact, on an inch-for-inch of body length basis, the oscar needs even more space than most other aquarium fishes, because it is a bulky species, not streamlined, and because it creates a lot of mess when it eats, both conditions being of a type to dictate the provision of extra space for the fish involved.

Under ideal conditions, a fish will be given as much tank space as it would require at its full size. That's the ideal, but it is rarely applied in actual practice. What usually happens is that the hobbyist takes a fancy to a fish and decides in his own mind what he can offer by way of accommodations as compared to what he thinks the fish actually needs... and then he buys the fish regardless of what he thinks it needs, hoping that all will go well even though he knows that he's not able to provide enough room. Let's face it: this is what happens. You can talk all day about how it's not sensible, how it's self-defeating in the long run, how it will result in sick fish and disappointment for their owner, how it's much better to wait until he can provide accommodations of the correct size, but he's going to do it anyway. For practicality's sake, then, let's just make a recommendation by way of stating a general guideline about how many gallons of tank capacity is advisable for each inch of oscar to be housed in the tank. A fair rule of thumb would be to provide $2\frac{1}{2}$ gallons of tank capacity for each inch of body (that is, length without counting the tail) length of oscar. Some will provide less space for their fish, and the fish, and consequently their owners, will suffer for it; some will provide more space, maybe much more, and profit from it, because there is no such thing as providing too much tank room for an oscar. The guideline is misleading in that it doesn't take the shape of the tank into consideration, and the shape of tank is important in determining its fish-holding capacity. Length and width of the tank determine its surface area, and surface area is mostly what counts, so a high tank having a greater gallonage capacity than a low tank but the same base dimensions wouldn't be able to house more oscars just because of its increased gallonage; the tank sold as a "20-gallon low" has the same base dimensions as the standard 29-gallon tank, for example, and can house as many oscars as the larger tank.

This guide assumes that the tank is filtered (it doesn't have to be aerated as well, because the filtation process will itself accomplish a good amount of aeration), and that partial water changes will be made on a regular basis. It of course also assumes that gross mismanagement in the form of heavy overfeeding, abrupt temperature changes and poisonings from metals or other potentially toxic substances introduced into the tank will be avoided. It also assumes that the oscar or oscars involved will be the only fish in the tank. This is really unrealistic in the sense that oscars, in their smaller sizes at least, may be put into tanks that contain other species. As the oscar grows, it will eliminate most tankmates that stay small, and tankmates that match it in growth shouldn't be housed with it in the first place if you want optimum growth for the oscar.

There are a few aquarium fishes that can be maintained in bowl-type and goblet-type aquaria over long periods of time without suffering any bad effects, but the oscar definitely is not one of them. Apart from the incongruity involved in housing an oscar in a set-up like the one pictured, there is also a certainty that any oscar so handled wouldn't live very long.

There's both good news and bad news in the guideline. Good news for new hobbyists who have very limited tank facilities but would like to own an oscar and have been told that they shouldn't own one unless they can provide a minimum of a 20-gallon tank. They can, provided they can content themselves with a small oscar. Bad news for those who think that they can raise *many* oscars to full or near-full size in a larger-than-normal tank. They can't.

If you want an oscar, you can have one, regardless of what size of tank you own; you just can't have one of the size you might want. If you have a small tank, you're stuck with small oscars, and that's that. Unfortunately, small oscars don't have the personality or true pet potential of adult or near-adult oscars. They may be a good deal more interesting than other fishes of comparable size, but they're not really oscary oscars. So in some respects it is a waste of good space to keep a single small oscar (or group of small oscars) when that same space could be more enjoyably used for the containment and study of fishes not requiring as much room. I think that even the most ardent oscar fancier would agree that a five-gallon tank could provide greater enjoyment to a hobbyist if it contained three pairs of guppies rather than a single small oscar.

When you get into the field of larger oscars, though, whatever space you expend is well worth it, so don't stint on size. If you have a 29-gallon tank and want to use it to house an interesting, attractive display fish, an adult oscar would be a perfect occupant. If you have a fifty gallon tank and would like the same thing, plus a chance to spawn a fish that comparatively few other hobbyists have spawned, oscars will give you your chance. It is important to remember that tank size plays a large role in determining not only the growth rate (and ultimate size) of fishes maintained in them but also in pro-

Florida fish farmers are able to keep oscars in outdoor pools such as this; because of the space available to the fish and the heavy feedings they receive, the oscars grow very quickly. Mature oscars breed in the pools, and the fish farmers are able to raise hundreds of thousands of marketable babies every year. Photo by Dr. Herbert R. Axelrod.

viding a margin of safety for them when conditions start to go bad. For example, it has been my experience with tropicals that in a large tank you have a lot more leeway for errors and unavoidable bad conditions than you have with a smaller tank, even when the smaller tank is not crowded to begin with. Let's say, for instance, that two pairs of rams, *Apistogramma ramirezi*, maintained in a ten-gallon tank (in which they wouldn't be crowded) could withstand a constant low temperature of 68° for two weeks before their health would suffer. In a twenty-gallon tank, the same rams would be able to withstand the same low temperature for a longer period, and they would be able to stand a lower temperature for the same period. The same applies to a lack of food; a fish could go longer without food in a fifty-gallon tank than in a twenty-gallon tank.

More important to remember, and unfortunately often overlooked by hobbyists, is the fact implicit in the guideline that a tank perfectly suitable for a fish at one period in its life won't be suitable when it has achieved growth. When your baby oscar has grown from two inches in length to five inches in length, make sure you take its increased size into consideration and give it increased tank space.

# 3.

# EQUIPMENT AND DECORATIONS FOR THE OSCAR TANK

## FILTRATION SYSTEMS

To a certain extent, the need for efficiency in filtration systems for use in tanks housing oscars is dictated by the size of the fish: if oscars need big tanks and big tanks need good filtration systems, oscar owners need good filtration systems. To a certain extent, the need is dictated by the habits of the fish, most especially its eating habits. The oscar happens to be a sloppy eater, even sloppier than other fishes of its size. Big oscars will chomp and gum and worry their food, and small particles get spit out and scattered all over the tank, where they can lie ignored, eventually to decompose. Decomposition processes going on in the tank are of course potentially very dangerous. Organic substances cannot safely be left lying around in the tank; choosing a filter thus becomes a job of picking out the unit that will remove most of the subject-to-decay organic materials in the tank without overdoing things by using a unit too powerful for the size of the tank to be filtered.

In a small tank, one up to 10 gallons in capacity, you can get by with a small filtration system, say an inside box filter or a small outside filter; even a good under-gravel filter can do the job, although large oscars and undergravel filtration systems don't match very well, one laribus serie dentium acutorum exsertorum armatum, pone quos fascia lata dentium velutinorum minimorum exstat. Ossa pharyngea superiora et inferiora latis fasciis dentium magnorum obtuse-conicorum apiceque subhamatorum armata. Linea lateralis interrupta. Pinna dorsalis longissima, antice aculeis acutissimis, apice cuticula appendiculatis, postice radiis articulatis sensim longiori-bus, et omnino squamatis suffulta. Pinna caudalis omnino squamata. Pinna analis antice acu-leis validissimis aucta, caeterum eandem praebet indolem, quam pars mollis pinnae dorsalis. Pinnae ventrales acuminatae, aculeo primo breviore; pectorales subrotundatae.

## 1. LOBOTES OCELLATUS Cuv. in litt. Tab. LXVIII.

Aculei pinnae dorsalis omnibus ejusdem longitudinis, excepto primo breviore; ocellis nigris alis marginatis ad basin pinnarum pectoralium pinnae dorsalis et in lobo superiore pinnae caudalis.

Caput crassissimum, obtusissimum, quartam partem totius longitudinis aequans. Operculum latum rotundatum, squamis illis trunci parum minoribus obtectum; praeoperculum laeve, alepido-tum, magnis foveis mucosis notatum. Membrana branchiostega tenuis, lata, pone operculum prominens. Apertura branchialis sat magna. Buccae intumidae, squamis parvis obsitae. Oculi magni pone et supra maxillarum commissuram siti. Nares utrinque simplices, pyriformes, me-diocres, inter oculos et rostri apicem intermediae. Plurima foramina mucosa, gregatim in sum-mo vertice, ad nares, et in ossibus infraorbitalibus aperiuntur. Os labris crassis cinctum; man-dibula crassa, latiuscula, prominens. Truncus latus, crassus, squamis subaequalibus, deciduis ad dorsi marginem et versus caudae apicem minoribus, tectus. Squamae omnes circulares, ma-xime regulares, lineis curvis concentricis confertissimis et radiis pluribus antrorsum divergentibus, et in marginem lobulatum decurrentibus notatae. Punctum radiationis in mediis squamis. Linea lateralis sursum flexa, cum dorso parallela, usque ad mediam pinnae dorsalis posterioris partem, inde interrupta, in medio caudae latere recta. Squamae ejus vix minores canali mucoso simplici, a media squama oriundo et in margine postico emarginato, aperto, insignes. Pinna dorsalis ultra medium aculeis validis, acutissimis, apice ut in Labris appendiculatis, postice radiis articu-latis, gracilibus, apice pluries fissis caudae apicem versus sensim majoribus et per totam longi-tudinem squamulis minimis obductis. Pinna caudalis rotundata, omnino squamulata; extus radiis minimis cuti immersis vix conspicuis, caeteris radiis pluries fissis suffulta. Pinna analis antice aculeis tribus brevioribus, validissimis, crassis, acutissimis, radiis sequentibus ejusdem indolis et formae quam illi partis mollis pinnae dorsalis. Aculeus primus pinnarum ventralium, radio se-quenti duplo brevior. Pinnae pectoralis radius primus brevis tenuis, parvus; sequentes radii plures et profunde fissi.

Dorsum virescens, venter et latera flavicantia.

Pinnae pectorales radiis 15, ventrales 6, analis 3, 16, caudalis intus 15, dorsalis 13, 20.

In Museo Monacensi specimen in spiritu vini servatur 10″ longum.

*Habitat in Oceano Atlantico.*

A page from the book containing Baron Cuvier's original scientific description of the oscar, then called *Lobotes ocellatus.*

Biological filtration is one of the most efficient ways of ridding an aquarium of unwanted ammonia which results from fish wastes. The conventional method of providing such filtration is to use an undergravel filter. However, because of the oscar's digging habits, an undergravel filter will not operate very efficiently. The alternative is to use a high-pressure gravel filter such as this one in which the biologically active gravel bed is contained within the filter.

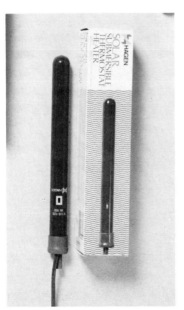

Thermostatically controlled heaters are available in sizes to suit almost any aquarium and are available also in submergible and non-submergible form. At left is a submergible heater, at right is a non-submergible heater, which is attached to the rim of the tank.

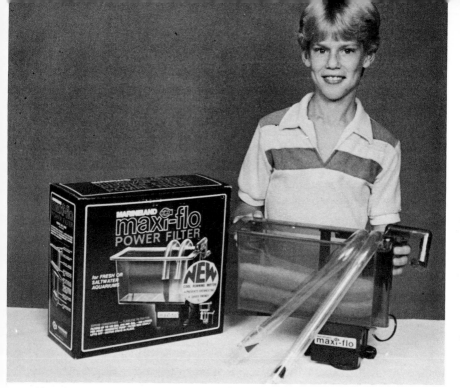

This type of filter is known as a power filter; power filters basically are small water pumps that circulate the water rapidly.

reason being that large oscars like to take the gravel on the bottom of a tank and shift it around to suit themselves, and this is totally destructive of the undergravel filtration system's efficiency.

Once you get into the range of larger oscars and correspondingly larger tanks, the best filtration is obtained by use of a power filter. Power filters push water directly rather than relying on an output of air to create a vacuum that lifts filtered water back into the tank, so they can filter more gallons per hour and therefore do a better filtering job on large tanks. Also, they create a current in the water that seems to be beneficial to the fish; other filters also produce a current, but much less strongly. If you are housing a big oscar in a big tank, a power filter is your best bet; if you are housing a number of large oscars in a big tank, or a greater number of small oscars, a power filter is almost necessary. I am not saying that oscars cannot be maintained without filtration; they can, but only by the exercise of great care and with extra work on their owners' parts. The extra work and care aren't really worth the effort, because a good filtration system doesn't cost that much and provides a nice margin of safety as well as being a work-saver and tank-beautifier.

One very important point as regards maintenance of good water quality for oscars (or any other fish) is this: make frequent partial changes of the water. This basic element in successful aquarium maintenance is not stressed as heavily as it should be; aquarium books do not place enough emphasis on it, fish dealers don't harp on it to their customers as much as they should, and exerienced hobbyists don't point it out to beginners as unfailingly as they should when passing along advice to beginners. But it is immensely important; I maintain that the making of frequent partial water changes is the single most important positive action an oscar owner can take to insure the good health of his fish. It improves color; it improves growth; it improves behavior; it helps the fish to resist disease; it keeps the tank cleaner and the water clearer; it promotes spawning readiness . . . in short, it has many beneficial effects and no drawbacks, other than that it takes a little time and effort. I don't care what kind of magnificently elaborate and efficient filtration system you use: nothing can take the place of frequent partial changes of water. Bear in mind that even the diatomaceous earth filters designed for aquarium use, efficient as they are, cannot remove dissolved waste products that pollute the water as a consequence of the fish's excretion; no aquarium filter can, regardless of how efficient it is when used in conjunction with even the finest activated carbons and charcoals. The fish's excretory products slowly poison the water and therefore slowly kill the fish; these poisons *must* be removed, and making frequent partial water changes is the best way to remove them. Use this as a formula: once a week, take 25% of the water out of the tank and discard it, replacing it with fresh water. It would be best if the water used in replacement has been aged a few days to give the dissolved gases it contains a chance to dissipate, but it's not strictly necessary. It should be close to the temperature of the water already in the tank, but don't worry about a few degrees' difference. The important thing is to GET THAT NEW WATER INTO THE TANK. Make the removal-replacement procedure a truly routine maintenance chore for your oscars and you will be adding a great deal to your enjoyment of them. While you're removing the old water, go over the bottom of the tank and pick up any uneaten foodstuffs.

## PLANTS AND DECORATIONS

Small oscars can be kept in planted aquaria, those that contain rooted plants, because small oscars usually don't bother plants. Large oscars usually can't be kept in planted aquaria, except extraordinarily large ones, because large oscars usually *do* bother plants. Large oscars bother rooted plants by turning them into uprooted plants. It doesn't make much difference whether the plants are small or large, planted in gravel or planted in special pots; if a large oscar wants to move them, and he usually will, he will. I have seen oscars that took a dislike to something in their tank far heavier than plants actually throw the offending object out of the tank, so it's not hard to see that even the largest Amazon sword plant wouldn't stand much chance against a big oscar. Give the fish its head; if you want rooted plants in the tank and the oscar leaves them alone, fine. But if you want rooted plants in the tank and the oscar seems to mind their presence to the degree that he pulls them up as fast as you put them down, give it up as a bad job and stop trying to put in rooted plants . . . unless you just want to provide entertainment for the fish or are interested in a protracted piscine-human contest of wills. If you insist on having some type of plant shape rising from the bottom of the tank, use plastic plants and anchor them down securely with heavy rocks; if you do the job right, your fish *might* not be able to move them.

Floating plants are a different story. Even big oscars usually won't bother floating plants (except, occasionally, to eat them), and since floating plants will help to cut down on the intensity of the light in the tank, they serve a good purpose, because oscars don't like to live in brightly lighted tanks. They prefer subdued lighting, and they look better under subdued lighting. Of course, you can achieve the subdued lighting effect by using a bulb of smaller wattage capacity, thereby doing away with any need for floating plants. Floating plants have one disadvantage in that they can provide a haven for small food animals in which to hide from the oscar.

Many oscar owners don't bother with plants at all for oscar tanks, using either totally bare tanks or tanks to which only rocks have been added. Bare tanks, of course, don't look good; they're fine for people who are keeping oscars in the cellar or someplace else where the tanks can be strictly functional, without any decorative effect at all, but they won't do for the showplace of a pet. Oscars owners who are concerned about the esthetic appeal of the oscar tank can use rockwork to good effect. Although there are quite a few rocks that can serve the purpose, being both available and decorative and not too expensive and not harmful from the standpoint of affecting the water quality adversely, various types of shale happen to be the rock choice of most oscar owners. It is the most common and least costly of all the rock types sold in aquarium stores, and it can be very attractive if arranged artistically in the tank. If you don't have either the talent or inclination to create shale arrangements for your tank, you can buy them ready-made. They come in the form of cliffs and ledges and caves, among other fabricated shapes, but probably the most popular of all are the shale rock backgrounds designed to cover the entire rear of a tank. Most of these backgrounds can be used inside or outside the tank, and they're quite attractive. They also are comparatively expensive. You can make your own shale backgrounds by chipping up the shale yourself and embedding it in a nontoxic cement, of course, or you can buy an imitation shale background done in plastic. If you don't want shale, you can have a Chinese temple scene or Roman gardens or the Battle of the Marne or whatever else happens to strike your fancy. If you like it and the oscar doesn't go into sulks over it, suit yourself; so long as whatever you put into the tank can't hurt the fish by being too sharp or toxic or providing a place for the build-up of pollution, no harm is done except possibly to the sensibilities of the more esthetically inclined and puristically nature-minded.

## HEATERS

The need for heating equipment depends partly on the temperatures in the area where you live and partly on your style of raising fishes, as well as on the size of the tank(s). Some hobbyists who raise oscars never have any real need for heating equipment, since the temperatures in their area never go low enough to require steady heating of the water. Oscars can get by at 70°F.

easily enough even though 70°F. would normally be considered too low for good growth. A temperature that remains a degree or two upward or downward of 76°F. would be much better, with breeding temperatures about 5 degrees higher than the average non-spawning temperature. In sub-tropical areas like Hawaii and southern Florida, oscars can be maintained outdoors permanently. In warmer temperate areas, which for our purposes here we'll define as those in which an unheated outdoor pool of a minimum of 500 gallons in capacity would not fall below 65°F. for more than a day or so during the summer, oscars can safely be kept outside; the large quarters thus afforded will do them a lot of good. Young oscars will grow much more quickly, with less attention, if maintained in a large outdoor raising pool, but they'll get a trifle ragged-looking.

In general, the best recommendation about the purchase of heating equipment is to get the best, or at least close to the best, and make sure that it is powerful enough to heat the biggest tank it may be used in. You might not need a heater at all if the place in which you keep the oscar tank wouldn't allow an unheated tank to fall below 68°F. for more than a day or so, but you would certainly need one if you wanted to raise the temperature to between 80° and 85° in a place that never goes much over 72°. Whatever type of heater you choose, make sure that it can be securely anchored in place; a large oscar can easily knock a loose heater out of the tank, a prospectively very dangerous situation. Completely submergible heaters are good but comparatively expensive.

## LIGHTING EQUIPMENT

Aquarium reflectors serve two major purposes: they provide light for live plants and light for the aquarist to see into the tank. If you don't have live plants in the tank, and it receives enough incidental light to enable you to see into it, you don't need an aquarium reflector at all, because oscars don't like bright light. If the oscar tank happens also to be a decorative feature of your house, you'll want it lighted, but don't let the light become glaring. Whether the lighting fixture is incandescent or fluorescent makes no difference to the fish, but red oscars show up best under the fluorescent fixtures designed for good plant growth.

## COVERS

Every oscar tank should be covered and kept covered. One reason is that although oscars aren't among the really insistent jumpers of the aquarium fish world, they are prone to making a sporadic leap or two, and you might as well be prepared. It's bad enough to lose an ordinary tropical because you failed to keep the tank covered, but it can be a lot worse to lose a real pet, especially a prospectively valuable one. Another reason is to keep dust and dirt out of the tank. Most hobbyists don't realize how much airborne dirt can eventually settle to the bottom of a fishtank, but it can be a considerable amount, and if it doesn't hurt in volume it can hurt in kind. Pesticidal sprays and other potentially deadly contaminants might be unknowingly put into the air around the oscar tank, and a tight-fitting cover can minimize the danger of having them settle into the water. Since contaminants like the chemicals in pesticidal sprays definitely will get into the tank one way or the other (mostly through the filtering system) if they are sprayed into the air around the tank, the presence of a cover might make the difference between life and death for your fish, just by cutting down on the amount of toxic material that does reach the water. Another reason is to prevent the fish from splashing you and objects around the tank. Oscars do like to splash water out of the tank, and a mature fish can do quite a bit of sprinkle work by whipping its broad tail around the top of the tank. With young oscars, you can avoid jumping and splashing by simply covering the tank, but with older, heavier fish you have to both cover it and weigh or clamp the cover down.

## ACCESSORIES

All of the little tools and gadgets used with tanks housing other species have value for oscar specialists, too. Thermometers, feeding rings, dip tubes (mechanized or manually operated), nets, siphons, pH and hardness test kits . . . they all have their place. Owners of large oscars need wide, deep nets of soft fibers, although some owners of big fish never use nets at all, doing whatever oscar-transfer work has to be done by trapping the fish in a soft towel or blanket after first removing most of the water in the tank. Thermometers and siphons are essential, but don't go overboard on the pH and water hardness testing equipment, if for no other reason than that using it might turn you into a water quality nut, and that's bad. Don't be too concerned about the pH of your water or its hardness; oscars will live and spawn in a wide range of pH-hardness conditions, and the main thing you have to watch out for is that changes in the make-up of the water aren't made too abruptly.

# 4.

# FEEDING OSCARS

Oscars, large and small, are big eaters. In fact, they are downright gluttonous. Sometimes their excesses in consumption give them serious digestive upsets; oscars even have been known to die as the result of eating too much.

## LIVE FISHES

In general, oscars like to eat live foods, especially fishes. But providing a steady diet of live fishes is an expensive proposition. If you can feed your oscar(s) fishes that you've raised yourself, you can of course keep the cash outlay for food fishes to the minimum, but you'll still have the expense in terms of tank space used to breed or house the food fishes. If you have to buy the fishes, it can run into good money . . . and you still have the tank space expense until the fishes are eaten, because you can't save much unless you buy in bulk quantities. In some areas, for example, you can buy 2-inch goldfish at 3 cents apiece if you buy them in lots of 100. If you buy in smaller lots, the price can go up to 10 cents or 15 cents apiece. Let's say that you have a 10-inch oscar that will eat three 2-inch goldfish a day. Your oscar therefore will cost you about $3 a month to feed if you feed it exclusively on goldfish.

That's a lot of money, much too much if you're counting on making a profit from the sale of an oscar, even though it's not too much to pay if you are treating the fish strictly as a pet and according it the special treatment its status as a pet demands. Also, where are you going to keep all those goldfish? You'd have to set up a special fish-holding container just to provide food. Additionally, you might recoil from the idea of feeding one living animal to another, at least if the food animal happens to be a fish or something higher on the taxonomic tree.

In general, live fishes are the best all-around food for oscars. They are nutritionally sound, easy and clean to feed, and almost always available. The major drawback in trying to feed oscars on a diet exclusively or almost completely consisting of live fishes is the cost. Unless you breed fishes in sufficient numbers to always have enough surplus and discards on hand to feed to your oscar(s), such a feeding regimen could run into big money. An additional drawback is that live fishes can carry parasites and diseases that could attack an oscar, and that's a danger that can't be brushed off.

Hobbyists having easy access to the ocean are fortunate, because the ocean provides a rich variety of marine life that oscars eagerly accept and thrive on. Various saltwater and brackish water killifishes of the kind that are sold for bait in coastal bait shops are excellent for oscars. You can catch your own and have a ready supply during the months that they are available for the taking. The same applies to clams, shrimps, and to a lesser extent, small crabs. Large crabs should be avoided entirely. But marine organisms of all kinds are in general much harder to maintain alive than freshwater food animals, and this detracts from their value.

Bodies of fresh water will of course provide many suitable foods for oscars, but freshwater organisms are much more potentially dangerous as regards transmission of diseases and parasites than marine organisms. Also, the collection of freshwater life of any type is in most places more closely regulated by law, and you have to be careful about what you collect. In any event, it seems almost shameful to collect fishes, whether fresh-water or saltwater, for the express purpose of feeding them to a pet. The same is true of gathering tadpoles and salamanders for use as food. Even crayfish (large oscars love to eat crayfish) seem to deserve better than to be taken from their stream for chomping by an oscar.

So although live fishes are the best food for oscars, it's not always possible or desirable to provide them as the staple item of diet. Therefore most oscar owners have to provide at least some portion of their oscars' diets in non-living form whether they want to or not. But before we explore the many non-living foods, let's run through a catalogue of the various live foods available at least seasonally from pet shops and tropical fish shops.

## LIVE FOODS NORMALLY AVAILABLE FROM AQUARIUM DEALERS

The four most commonly available live foods sold exclusively for use by aquarium hobbyists are tubifex worms, brine shrimp, daphnia and bloodworms. These foods vary greatly in price and in their degree of availability; they also differ greatly in their suitability for use as oscar food.

### Tubifex Worms

Tubifex worms are the most often available of aquarium live foods and the cheapest, and I think that they are definitely the best buy for putting growth on your fish at the lowest cost. Tubifex worms are suitable for oscars of all sizes (big oscars take them only in globs and will not bother with individual worms, but that's no problem) but are especially useful for putting size on young oscars. You might have heard that tubifex worms

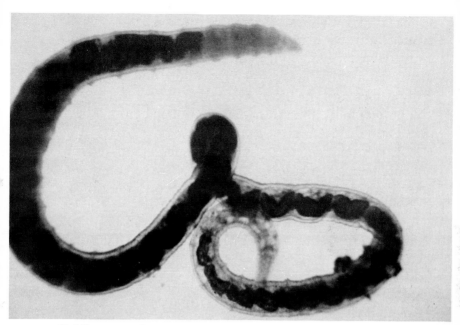

Tubifex worm. Photo by Dr. Rolf Geisler.

transmit all kinds of diseases to the fish that eat them and cause everything from whirling disease to fallen arches, but if you want to feed your oscars live foods at least occasionally you are sooner or later going to rely on tubifex worms; if you go about using them the right way, you'll have no problem.

The first point to consider is to make sure that the worms are good when you buy them. Unfortunately, some dealers don't store their worms properly, and once in a while they get stuck with a bad batch, too. Look at the worms before you buy them. If there is water above the worms in the container in which they are offered to you and that water is tinged pink or red, pass them by, because the worms are all or almost all dead and of no use to you. If there's no water above the worms but a glance at the container shows that you are being offered either a soupy gray or soupy red mass, pass them by for the same reason. Good live worms will be recognizable by the fact that you can see the movement of individual worms in the portion, and the water around them will be clear. Use worms a few times and you'll quickly be able to tell a good portion from a bad one, and you'll never get stuck.

The second thing to do is to clean the worms before you use them. The best way to clean them is to put them into a plastic bag, fill the bag about two-thirds full of cold water, give the neck of the bag a few twists to make it watertight, and then shake the bag vigorously to separate the worms from the effluvium that every portion of worms contains. (The live worms congregate in balls, or clumps, and each clump contains a bunch of garbage. The shaking operation is designed to separate the garbage from the worms.) After the first shaking operation, there will be a period of a few moments during which the effluvium will float at the surface or remain suspended in the water, above the worms, which settle quickly to the bottom. During this period, pour off as much of the water as you can, even if you lose a few worms. Go through the shaking and pouring operation three or four more times. Fill the bag as before once more and check to see how much suspended matter remains after an additional shaking. There shouldn't be much, and the worms should now look very different at the bottom of the bag. They should be reddish in color, and you should easily be able to distinguish the movements of individual worms. The water around them should be clear, not pink or gray. If, after all your shaking and pouring, there is a soupy looking mess at the bottom of the bag instead of a mass of squirming and obviously healthy worms, you bought a bad lot of worms and might as well throw the mess away. But if your worms were good in the first place and you went through the cleaning operations as described, you should have a good supply of fish-tempting live food that is the meat and potatoes of the aquarium world.

Depending on how many worms you bought and how many fish you have to feed, you might have to store the worms for a few days. Dealers and hobbyists who use worms in commercial quantities often store their worms in open pans under a constant trickle of running or dripping cold water. This keeps the worms alive and gives them a chance to be purged of whatever junk is in their systems (which no amount of shaking will remove). But for the small-scale hobbyist, this practice is very wasteful of water and in many cases not practical at all. The best place to store small amounts (say a portion or two) of tubifex worms is in the refrigerator, and the best way to keep them from going bad is to store them with as little water as possible.

Regardless of what type of container you store them in, don't have water above them; try to keep the refrigerated worms as free of excess water as you can. And the next time you feed them, repeat the cleaning process. Small portions of worms should be good for at least four days, possibly as long as a week, if the cleaning and storing processes detailed here are followed. But when the worms start to go bad, don't gamble; throw them out and get a new batch.

Live tubifex worms introduced as food into an aquarium soon separate and go their own way. If a tank has gravel on the bottom, they'll dig into it and establish themselves in it. If you want to get rid of any worms thus entrenched at the bottom of the tank, obtain a crayfish. There is no more efficient remover of tubifex worms than a crayfish ... and there is hardly any more appealing a dish to an oscar than a crayfish, so you'd better make sure that any crayfish introduced to an oscar tank for its capacities as a worm-eater is too big to be eaten itself. Big oscars eagerly take live crayfish as a food, spitting the pieces of shell all over the tank.

## Brine Shrimp

Live adult brine shrimp, often obtainable in pet shops, are a very good food for small and medium oscars; large oscars will take brine shrimp, too, but sometimes only half-heartedly, most probably because they are relatively small for such a big fish. Brine shrimp is a nutritious food that puts good growth on the fishes that eat it, and it has the advantage of not being contaminable by the usual freshwater fish diseases, as it is a strictly marine animal. But it is a very high-priced item and therefore not to be considered as a large part of the diet of any oscar, large or small. A portion of live brine shrimp will cost roughly the same as a portion of live tubifex worms but will contain only about one-twentieth as much real meat, since the greatest bulk of the portion by far consists of salt water in which the little shrimp live.

## Daphnia

Daphnia are freshwater crustaceans, much smaller than brine shrimp and a good deal less nutritious. They are a lot of fun to feed to small oscars but are not very sensible for large oscars, which often will ignore them entirely because of their small size. They also are very expensive, much too expensive to try to use as a staple in the diet, being priced about the same as a portion of tubifex or brine shrimp and containing far less real food value than either the worms or shrimp. They're good for an occasional treat but that's about it. Portions of live daphnia often contain various fish enemies such as hydras and predaceous insect larvae, too.

An adult brine shrimp, a male in this case, as can be noted from the large clasping claws at the crustacean's head. Live adult brine shrimp are a good but relatively expensive food.

Newly hatched brine shrimp nauplii. These infant crustaceans are the mainstay food of newly hatched oscars; they can be hatched from eggs packaged commercially and made available to tropical fish hobbyists. Frozen newly hatched brine shrimp also are available, but the frozen nauplii are less eagerly accepted by the baby fish.

A culture of microworms. Microworms are a good food for newly hatched oscars. Photo by Robert Gannon.

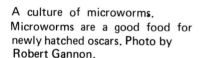

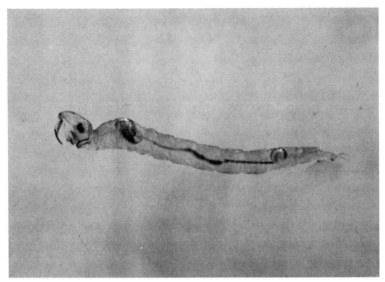

*Above:* glass worm; live or frozen, glass worms are good food for small and medium-size oscars. *Below:* closeup of a female freshwater crustacean of the genus *Daphnia.*

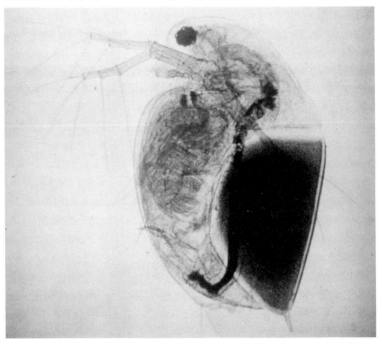

A bloodworm, larvae of the midge *Chironomus.* Photo by Dr. Rolf Geisler.

## Bloodworms

Live bloodworms, which are the least commonly obtainable of the four major aquarium live foods, are an excellent food for oscars or any other fish big enough to eat them. Bloodworms (genus *Chironomus*) are insect larvae, not worms; the "blood" part of their name comes from their color, which usually is a good solid red, and the "worm" part derives from their twitchy motion in the water. Oscars love them. They're too expensive to be a major part of the diet, but they are one of the few live foods worth collecting from local lakes and ponds. You might also catch another larval insect with a wormy name: the glass worm, which is the larva of a midge, *Chaoborus.* Glass worms also are very good food.

**Other live foods sold in the aquarium trade**

There are many other live foods for fishes offered for sale to aquarium hobbyists, but most are not available at tropical fish stores on a regular basis; some are almost never available and have to be ordered through mail-order sellers. Check the advertisements in each monthly issue of *Tropical Fish Hobbyist* magazine; you'll usually find an assortment of starting cultures of nine or ten different live foods from wingless fruit flies to micro-worms. The best thing about these foods is that once you have obtained a starting culture you can keep your supply going almost indefinitely. Most of them, however, are useful primarily for only the smallest oscars. Check a good book like Robert Gannon's *Live Foods* to determine the specific advantages to you of these hard-to-buy but useful live foods.

## OTHER LIVE FOODS

Besides the live foods that are customarily obtained from tropical fish stores, there are a number of other live foods that oscars will readily eat. Some of them are easy to obtain, whereas others are hard to get. Some are easy to get in some places but hard to get in other places. Take live crayfish, for example. They are an excellent food for big oscars and are obtainable in goodly number in many parts of the United States and other countries. But they are not available everywhere even in those countries in which they do exist, so not everyone who wants to can use them. The use of live marine and brackish water fishes, crustaceans and molluscs is another example. If you live near the ocean, fine, but if you don't live near the ocean you might as well forget about using them because you won't be able to obtain them alive . . . at least not without spending an arm and a leg to get them. There are many different live

# THE WORLD'S LARGEST SELECTION OF PET, ANIMAL, AND MUSIC BOOKS.

T.F.H. Publications publishes more than 900 books covering many hobby aspects (dogs, cats, birds, fish, small animals, music, etc.). Whether you are a beginner or an advanced hobbyist you will find exactly what you're looking for among our complete listing of books. For a free catalog fill out the form on the other side of this page and mail it today.

. . CATS . . .

. . . BIRDS . .

. . . ANIMALS . . .

. . . DOGS . . .

. . FISH . . .

. . . MUSIC . . .

For more than 30 years, *Tropical Fish Hobbyist* has been the source of accurate, up-to-the-minute, and fascinating information on every facet of the aquarium hobby.

Join the more than 50,000 devoted readers worldwide who wouldn't miss a single issue.

LOBOTES ocellatus

Tab.LXVIII

The color drawing that accompanied Cuvier's description; the body shape is correct for that of a mature oscar, but the colors are inaccurate, and the teeth are greatly exaggerated.

foods available for the catching, and all of them make satisfactory oscar food, but almost all of them have drawbacks of one kind or another that make their use either limited or inadvisable. For example, live fishes are good but not always obtainable and are possible transmitters of disease to the oscars; crayfish and other crustaceans (saltwater crustaceans included) are not always obtainable and are not good as a steady diet; water beetles and other insects, both adult and larval stages, can be more trouble than they're worth, although oscars accept many forms with gusto; molluscs can be very messy and are hard to keep alive, so you can't stock up on them. Aquarium snails are an exception in this regard, of course, and snails make good oscar food. Red ramshorns are especially good. You can keep a culture of them going in a small tank and drop in a few crushed ones to the oscar once in a while.

Shown is the red ramshorn snail, *Planorbis corneus,* a thin-shelled species that is especially useful. Photo by Milan Chvojka.

Of all the foods that can be captured easily at no real cost to you, the earthworm is far and away the best. Earthworms are easy to catch, and if you don't want to catch them yourself you can always buy them easily enough; they're easy to store if you can keep them cool, and they're very nutritious. In addition, they're easy to feed to the fish. Big and middle-size oscars accept whole worms, even the big ones, as they are, without any chopping or cutting up; small oscars are better off with worms that have been halved or quartered, and even though the job of chopping up worms isn't the most pleasant way to spend your time, it's not that bad. Just be glad that you're keeping oscars and not a community of really small fishes, for chopping up the worms into bite-size chunks for guppies and neon tetras can be a truly messy operation. Earthworms make excellent subjects for home culture, too, so you can keep your

Two types of earthworms: the smaller worms are the common garden earthworms of the northeastern United States, and the larger worms are nightcrawlers. Both are excellent foods for oscars, the larger worms being more suited to larger fish. Photo by Paul Imgrund.

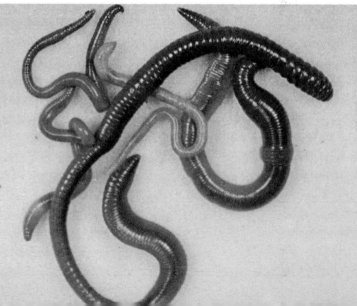

Mature oscars maintained in very large tanks have less inclination to uproot plants, although at spawning time they will clear the area near the egg site of all plant growth. Photo by *Straits Times,* Singapore.

Although this is not a representative of the strain sold as the red oscar, it has more red in it than normally appears in the regular oscar type. Photo by Dr. Herbert R. Axelrod.

supply going year-round with not very much effort on your part, and you don't have to make repetitive collecting expeditions. I believe that earthworms are the best all-around oscar food for the person who wants to provide a substantial part of the diet in live form and wants to avoid having to catch or buy his live food supplies at regular intervals.

## FROZEN FOODS

Daphnia, brine shrimp, bloodworms, mosquito larvae, beefheart, and a few other foods are available regularly in tropical fish stores in frozen form. Frozen brine shrimp is the most common and easily obtainable, and it can be a good food. It's comparatively expensive, but a given amount of frozen brine shrimp costs a lot less than the same number of live brine shrimp would, so the little crustaceans are a good deal more economical to feed in frozen form than alive. Frozen bloodworms also can be very good; again, like the brine shrimp, they are less expensive in frozen form than they are in live form. Frozen daphnia is pretty junky stuff for oscars, not worth while purchasing except as a last resort.

Frozen beefheart and other slaughterhouse by-products, which can be bought in large packages and therefore economical to use, has a good food value and is used as a staple item in the diet of oscars (and other tropicals) by many successful hobbyists; some, in fact, use practically nothing else. I find it to be messy and don't use it, but don't let my views prejudice you against a food that others rely on as a matter of course; give it a try and see how it fits into your scheme of doing things.

Apart from the cost, there is one big problem with feeding frozen foods: sometimes frozen foods get thawed out somewhere along the line between the packer and you, and instead of a package of frozen brine shrimp or bloodworms you get a package of re-frozen glop that once was frozen brine shrimp or bloodworms. Thawed out and re-frozen food is worse than worthless, it's prospectively harmful, and you have to be careful. Check the frozen food by dipping a small chunk of it in water to see what happens; if the the animals that form the basis of the food stay in individual units as they drop through the water, they should be all right, but if the chunk dissolves as a sort of amorphous gray mass of juices and pieces of animals rather than almost completely whole animals, watch out.

## AQUARIUM FOODS OTHER THAN LIVE OR FROZEN

In addition to live foods and frozen foods there are many packaged foods on the aquarium market. Most of these are dry foods, but some are in a semi-moist paste form. The dry foods (which include the freeze-dried foods) come in pellet, granule, tablet, flake and chunk forms. They vary in their ease of usage, cost, nutritive value, storability and other factors, but in the main are a good cheap food source for tropical fishes. Unfortunately, oscars are not typical of the main run of aquarium fishes, and some prepared foods just don't suit them when they get large. For small oscars, a variety of packaged dry foods, especially the meaty foods, can form the bulk of the diet, but big oscars will need chunkier items. Some owners of large oscars feed their fish regularly on pelleted dry foods, using mostly pellets that are designed for either pool fishes like goldfish and koi or hatchery-raised fish like trout. Although these pelleted foods are formulated specifically for good growth and health of the cyprinid and salmonid species for which they're intended, they do have a value when used as oscar food, and some people use them without

A mature red oscar, one of the individuals produced early in the existence of the red oscar strain. In individuals of more recent development, the red has been intensified. Photo by Dr. Herbert R. Axelrod.

Oscars generally are good parents and if left undisturbed will tend their young with diligence, even though the fry are sometimes pesky in their actions, swarming continually around their parents. The fry in this photo appear to have been fed on baby brine shrimp, as a pink flush typical of the flush appearing on the belly area of fry fed on newly hatched brine shrimp is visible on many of the fry, and the minute specks in the water appear to be being preyed on by the baby fish. Baby oscars show different rates of growth, and the faster growers in any given brood will eat their smaller siblings if given a chance. Photo by E.A. Baumbach.

Frozen foods aren't as much fun to feed as live foods, but they're in much more dependable supply. Pet shops now offer such a large variety of frozen fish foods that oscar owners can provide their fish with a highly varied diet.

any problem. But not all oscars will accept them, so try to obtain and use only a sample supply before you stock up on them.

## OTHER FOODS

Most hobbyists who go in for oscars in a big way and don't want or can't use live foods eventually hit upon the use of a variety of foods intended for consumption by human beings and pets other than oscars. These people-foods and pet-foods are generally cheap and easily available, and they fill the bill nicely. Among the people-type foods used for oscars are all kinds of fish and shellfish both fresh and frozen, and cheap (and some not-so-cheap) cuts of meat. The fish and shellfish have the advantage of being easier to use and cleaner and safer in that they do not contain any meat fats to foul up the water; they certainly are a more natural food for a fish than various cuts of beef would be. But unless you're able to obtain the right kinds of seafood, meat can actually be cheaper than fish. If you have a freezer and also happen to be a fisherman, you have a perfect combination, because you can freeze all types of fishes that you catch yourself and feed them to your oscar as needed. You don't even have to be a very successful fisherman, because you can use fillets of species that normally would be thrown away . . . even left-over bait fishes.

In the fish and shellfish departments, the only items you should avoid are oily fishes like smelts and tough-to-chew items like squids; clams and mussels also can present problems by messing up the water if they're not used properly and if they're not absolutely fresh. When using bivalve molluscs as oscar food, use only the solid muscular "foot" portion of the animals; don't use any of the softer parts, and don't under any circumstance make the mistake of slitting the molluscs into open-shell

Above and opposite, three fishes belonging to the same family as the oscar but differing greatly in morphological characters and behavior. Above, the ram, *Apistogramma ramirezi*; opposite, top: the jewel fish, *Hemichromis bimaculatus;* opposite, below, the angelfish, *Pterophyllum scalare,* the most popular of all cichlids.

Photo by H. J. Richter

halves and dropping them into the tank with soft parts and juices.

In the meat department, beefheart and beef liver are the staple items, although other beef products also are used. In preparing the heart and liver, you have to remove the tough, fibrous tissue; this task is less difficult and messy than it sounds, but it's still not a lot of fun. Some successful oscar raisers swear by beefheart and liver and have beautiful fish to back up their claims as to these foods' benefits, but I think that fish and shellfish are much better when all advantages and drawbacks are considered. Raw hamburger meat is often used to feed oscars, but I think it is best avoided, since it's greasy.

A number of oscar owners like to make up their own blends of food and then refrigerate the blended foods for easy availability as needed. Some do it to save money, some do it because they feel that they can thereby provide their oscars with a much more well balanced diet than would otherwise be provided, and some do it because they like to slop around.

Home blends of oscar food usually contain meat, fish, shellfish meat, cereal, leafy green vegetable fibers (spinach is a favorite), and some type of vitamin fortifier, all combined into a kind of pasty consistency. If you want to experiment with something like this, go ahead. You can find an excellent home-blender food recipe in *The Handbook of Tropical Aquarium Fishes,* by Drs. Axelrod and Schultz. Just remember that the oscar is a messy eater and that food that has a tendency to break down into small particles while being chewed by it is a prospective troublemaker in the tank because of the danger of decomposition of uneaten particles.

Dog and cat foods in both canned and kibbled form are popular oscar foods; the chunk-style canned foods

The bulging bellies of these two young oscars give proof of the bountiful feedings that they have received. It is much better to feed oscars small portions at frequent intervals than large portions at sporadic intervals, and it should be remembered that both young and old oscars have a tendency to be gluttonous: if they are fed too much at one time, they'll eat too much at one time. Photo by Dr. Herbert R. Axelrod.

are taken more readily by the fish but are much messier than the kibble types.

Part of the reason behind the great variety of food-stuffs offered to oscars lies in the fish's non-picky eating habits, and part lies in its size. If the oscar were a more finicky eater, hobbyists wouldn't be able to get away with offering weirdo diets, and if it were smaller and less of a heavy eater they wouldn't have to try.

Red oscars. In the photo at the bottom of the opposite page can be seen one of the small goldfish which formed the main food of these oscars. Photos by Dr. Herbert R. Axelrod.

# 5.

# BREEDING OSCARS

## OBTAINING A PAIR

Given a mature male and female and a big enough tank, it is not too tough to get oscars to spawn. Many have done it simply by providing the room and letting nature take its course. The hardest part about breeding oscars is making sure that you have a pair and giving them the requisite space in which to spawn.

As far as making sure you have a pair is concerned, the standard practice followed with many other aquarium fishes, to obtain between half a dozen and a dozen young fish and let them grow up together, hoping that the mathematical probability of there being at least one pair among the fish so chosen will be high, is tough to follow with a fish as big as mature oscars are. You just have too much space to devote to their keeping and too long to wait. Oscars won't spawn much before they're about six inches long, which should be when they're about 1 ½ years old, and tying up all that tank space for 1 ½ years can be trying on the prospective oscar breeder. Most hobbyists don't want to wait that long, so they have to cast about for alternative methods of obtaining breeding-size oscars. If money is no problem, it's easy: all you have to do is buy two obviously fully mature oscars and hope that they're a pair and that if they are a pair, that they're a compatible pair. This latter point is important, because oscars can be choosy about their mates. Although they are polygamous and willing to switch mates and spawn on the basis of availability, not every male is compatible with every female, regardless of how good the conditions you provide. At least, not every male is compatible with every female at the time you want them to be compatible. A prospective spawning partner might be ignored or fought with four times in a row and then spawned with successfully on the fifth attempt . . . but those first four failures can be frustrating. There would be no problem at all if oscars were able to be sexed reliably, because then all you would have to do would be to raise one good mature fish, determine its sex, and then scout up a partner of the opposite sex (or choose one from the others you might have raised). Unfortunately, sexing oscars reliably from strange stock just cannot be done. You can't do it on the basis of finnage or markings, you can't do it on the basis of behavior, and you can't do it on the basis of size, so you've struck out on three of the criteria that come in very handy in sexing many other species.

You might have read or been told that the mature male oscar has a number of spots at the base of his dorsal fin that the female does not have, and you might proceed to obtain mature fish that show these differences between one another, figuring to set them up and wait for them to spawn after you've given them the best of conditions. And you might be very sadly disappointed when nothing at all happens, because the presence or lack of markings on the dorsal fin is just not that reliable. Some males have them and some males don't, and the same applies to females. Mature males are sometimes said to be more colorful and more belligerent than mature females; some are, some aren't. Even if size were a completely reliable barometer of sex between fish of the same age, you could use it only with fishes whose age you knew for sure. Size can be as much a product of feeding and tank accommodations given the fish as of sex, and

Baby oscars of the regular strain. Photo by Harald Schultz.

Artist's conception of a mature oscar.

An adult oscar of the regular color pattern. Photo by Klaus Paysan.

so can color ... distinctions like this should not be followed blindly, or you'll end up wasting a lot of time. Additionally, it can be dangerous to count on a difference in size as a sure guide to sex, because oscars have a tendency to bully one another, and a much smaller oscar cooped up with a larger one in a tank intended for breeding can get badly mauled or even killed.

Let's cover three specific situations and develop what I consider to be sensible recommendations about how to obtain a male oscar and a female oscar to breed. In the first situation, you have only one fish; you are pretty sure from the size of the fish or what you know or think is its age (say a *minimum* of five and a half inches and a *minimum* of two and a half years) that it is breedable, but you don't know its sex. Since you don't know the sex of the other oscars you might see, either, you have to cast around a little bit and trust to luck. Breedable oscars aren't cheap, and you don't want to keep repeatedly trying without success, so it will pay you to keep the number of introduced prospective mates as small as possible. The first thing you should do is to try to find someone in your area who maintains that he has a good record of success in sexing oscars. This person, who may be either an experienced local aquarist (perhaps a member of an aquarium society to which you belong, in which case he'll be more inclined to help you) or a dealer, may be dead wrong about his ability to differentiate the sexes in oscars, but you still have nothing to lose in letting him pick a mate for your fish ... and if he's right you can be saving yourself a lot of trouble and expense. Let him see your fish, and then let him give or sell you one of his own or pick out one from someone else's stock. Take the hoped-for mate home and, after observing all commonsense aquarium practice precautions such as avoiding temperature differentials, etc., put it into the tank with your oscar.

But make sure that the tank has been partitioned beforehand so that the two oscars can see one another but not get at each other. If the two oscars indeed constitute a pair, this enforced separation will make them more compatible when they finally do get together. Feed them well while they're separated (a week's separation is about right), and gradually raise the temperature to 83°, keeping it at that point after you've removed the partition. Then observe what happens. If nothing happens and the fish just ignore one another, it could be that they're not a pair, but it also could be that they are a pair but are not ready to spawn, in which case you might want to try the partitioning treatment again. If nothing happens after the second partitioning and re-introdution, get a new mate for yours. You may be acting too hastily, but you don't want to spend too much time in coaxing a reluctant pair-that-might-not-be-a-pair, either.

If nothing as satisfying as egg-laying happens but the fish engage in a lot of jaw locking and head-to-tail quivering and tail-slapping, coupled with some very exciting gravel-moving (if there is gravel in the tank) or rock-cleaning (if there are rocks in the tank), you're probably on the right track. Give fish that act this way a day to consummate their pre-spawning roughhouse and housekeeping activities, but if they haven't spawned within a day or so after beginning them, partition them once more. After the second partitioning and re-rendezvous, they should get down to business. But if they don't, don't be too hasty to get rid of the fish you obtained. Give the pair at least one more chance before splitting them up permanently.

If the fish are openly antagonistic to one another, with one obviously trying to punish the other by biting and butting in the mid-section and around the head, and one fish succeeds in more or less cornering its tankmate,

Aquarium snails can provide variety and nutriment in the diet of oscars. For smaller oscars, the snails should be crushed and dropped into the tank; larger oscars will do their own shell-crushing.

Whether the tank is bare or decorated, oscars usually will spawn on some type of fairly smooth rock surface provided for the purpose; the rock surface may be laid flat, angled or even raised to provide a platform, as shown above. If no spawning rock is provided, the spawn may be deposited right on the bottom of the tank after the parents have removed gravel or similar covering layer over the spawning area. If the spawning tank is an all-glass tank, it is best to provide a spawning slate, as the glass bottom is less likely to be used as a site of deposit for the eggs. Photo by Husein Rofe.

returning every once in a while to deliver a bite or butt, split them up and partition them again. They might be a pair, but most likely they're not; even if they are, they're not ready to spawn. Spawning play among oscars is usually accompanied by a good deal of piscine agonistic behavior, but it's not vicious, and the struggle doesn't become lopsided, with one fish doing all the punishing and the other continuously on the receiving end. If after they've been partitioned and put together again, no improvement is seen in their behavior, keep your fish and return the other one. They're not going to spawn.

A telltale sign that a given oscar is ready to spawn is the emergence of its "spawning tube," which is the ovipositor or egg chute on the female and sperm chute on the male. The female's tube is broader and blunter than the male's, because the comparatively large eggs have to pass through it. If you observe the protrusion of the spawning tube on any of the fish in any of the situations described above, don't be too quick to give up on your chances of eventually being able to obtain a spawn, regardless of how the fish behave when first introduced.

In the second situation, you have at least two fish of your own that you consider to be a breedable size. You can then just follow the procedure outlined above, but you can take more time, because you don't have to return any fish. You can just keep trying the various combinations (if you have more than two fish) in succession until you find one of them that works. If you have three fish, the odds are good that from the three of them you'll be able to produce a pair. The larger the number of fish you have, the necessarily greater the chances of obtaining at least one pair; with nine fish, for example, you have almost a mathematical certainty that you will have at least one pair. This fact is the single greatest advantage, as far as success in breeding oscars is concerned, in raising your own breeding stock from young fish you acquire. Not many hobbyists, though, are able to use the system, because of the demands in tank space that such a group of spawning candidates would make.

The third situation would be one under which you have no oscars at all and must start from scratch to obtain a pair. You can either buy a group of mature oscars at random or buy (or rent) what someone may claim to be a guaranteed mated pair. Now a guaranteed mated pair is a pair that has proved that they're a pair by spawning and producing fry; it is not a pair that is necessarily guaranteed to spawn for you. The seller or renter guarantees their sexual status, not their breedability by you. I personally don't think much of the idea of someone's going out cold into the world of oscars and trying to obtain a pair to breed, but it's been done before and will continue to be done as long as hobbyists want to breed oscars and don't want to invest the time and space required to obtain their own stock. It's not done too often, though, mostly because there are not that many breeders of oscars willing to sell, give away or rent their fish out. In fact, there are not that many breeders of oscars, willing or unwilling. In fact, there are not that many owners of mature oscars. Unless you have a legitimately pressing reason for wanting a guaranteed mating pair, it's not a very satisfying course to pursue. There might be a considerable expense involved, without any guarantee of success, for one thing; additionally, you miss the undeniably pleasurable sensation of being honestly able to say that you raised the parents to parenthood all by yourself. Just in case you do feel that your interests are best served by waiving all the fooling around and starting out with a supposedly guaranteed mated pair, make sure that you get all details of payments straightened out beforehand. Have concrete

Large oscars can safely be housed with big *Anostomus* and *Leporinus* species and with large catfishes like *Sorubim* and *Pimelodus*. In general, oscars will get along well with other large fishes if those fishes are not overly aggressive and territory-minded. Depending on the individual fish concerned, they also can be kept with other large cichlids. But tank size plays a very large part in determining whether oscars and other fishes will get along well on a live-and-let-live basis; in tanks from fifty gallons on up, the mixed species become more compatible, whereas they have more of a tendency to fight among themselves as the swimming space available to them decreases.

*Pseudoplatystoma fasciatum.* Here is one catfish that could easily turn the tables on an oscar, even a big one, for it is a large fish with a big mouth and a big appetite. Photo by Klaus Paysan.

agreements hammered out as to such questions as:

What happens if one or both of the fish die within a week of your obtaining them?

What happens if one or both of the fish are damaged while in your care (for rental agreements only)?

What happens if the fish don't spawn?

What happens if the fish do spawn but the eggs are infertile?

Just to forestall questions on the part of readers of this book who have somehow gotten the idea that there is some intrinsic value to a mated pair of oscars, let me say right now that there is no such thing as a "fair" price for them. Oscars, like everything else, are worth what a seller can get for them without putting a gun to a buyer's head; their fair price is anything a mentally competent and uncoerced buyer is willing to pay. If you want to find out how much you'd have to pay to obtain a pair of mated oscars, ask around in your neighborhood, which is an entirely different thing from asking what a mated pair are "worth."

## THE SPAWNING PROCESS

Thus far we haven't covered the actual mechanics of oscar reproduction, so let's do it now. Oscars reproduce in this way: the female lays eggs, and the male fertilizes them. Given the proper conditions, tiny fry will emerge from almost all of the fertilized eggs. Some of these fry will die almost immediately, some will linger a few days and then die, some will stay alive for a few weeks or months and then die, and some will survive to maturity. In nature, probably upwards of 90% of the fry will die before they're an inch long; a good percentage of the remainder will die some time before they reach maturity. No one knows the mortality rates for wild oscars of various ages; they don't matter anyway, because what goes on in nature and what goes on in the

A pair of about-to-spawn oscars going through one of their pre-spawning maneuvers. Here the fish are aligned side by side and are slapping each other with their tails, mouths opened wide. Notice that this action is taking place directly above the flat rock eventually chosen as the spot for depositing the eggs. Photo by Jukka Jarvi.

Crayfish look menacing, but they're no match for grown oscars, which eat them greedily. Crayfish are interesting aquarium inhabitants themselves and are the best removers of live tubifex worms that have become entrenched in the aquarium gravel. Photo by Dr. Herbert R. Axelrod.

Shrimp; all types of shrimp, both freshwater and marine species, are good food for oscars.

Getting down to the important business of spawning, both members of the pair engage themselves in cleaning the rock. At this point, the genital papillae of the fish have already emerged partly, but the fish still can't be sexed with certainty. Photo by Jukka Jarvi.

Well matched oscar pairs are usually prolific breeders. A fully matured pair that has bred at least a few times can produce over 1,000 young in a single brood. As soon as they become free-swimming, baby oscars tend to swarm closely around one or both parents. Photos by E.A. Baumbach.

Having deposited a group of eggs on the rock, the female oscar backs off a little, cocking her mobile eyes to survey her handiwork. Her broad, blunt ovipositor is clearly visible. Photo by Jukka Jarvi.

At intervals during the spawning, the partners take time out for lip-locking engagements. The center of the egg mass is clear of eggs because the male of the pair destroyed them. Photo by Jukka Jarvi.

After all the eggs had been laid, the parents took up the guard position, jockeying with one another to determine which one would be closest to the eggs. Only half of the eggs from this spawning were fertilized. Photo by Jukka Jarvi.

Appearing on the opposite page is a photo of a natural jungle habitat in which oscars can be found. The photo was taken by Dr. Herbert R. Axelrod near Tefe in Brazil. The artificial environment shown above is quite similar to the natural environment of the oscar. Although the large schilbeid catfishes in this tank are an African species, they will do well in an aquarium containing oscars. Photo by Dr. D. Terver, Nancy Aquarium, France.

aquarium are entirely different things. You're going to lose a lot of young fish from any spawning, but you should be able to do much better by your oscars than nature does.

Before the eggs are laid, male and female go through a more or less ritualized series of pre-spawning motions that may consist of jaw-locking, tail-slapping, chasing and retreating, nipping, threatening, nudging, rolling over . . . you name it. It may consist of all these things, a few of them, or (very rarely) none of them. Interspersed with the pre-spawning ritual, which may last from just a few minutes to over a day, will be periods during which either or both fish settle down to some cleaning of the area which will be the eventual site for depositing the eggs. The area will get a good scrubbing by the fish's mouth. The site for the eggs may be either the bottom of the tank itself or a piece of rockwork in the tank. The rockwork may be either natural, such as a fairly flat piece of shale, or manufactured, such as a slab of slate. If the bottom of the tank is covered with gravel, the fish will clear the gravel away and create a bare spot; they never lay their eggs directly on the gravel. After the egg site has been cleaned to their satisfaction, the female will deposit the eggs. The eggs will be laid in strings or rows that follow a generally round pattern; that is, the pattern of the egg mass when finally laid will be roughly circular. There is no completely orderly arrangement of the eggs, and about the only thing you can count on is that no egg will be laid on top of a previously laid egg. The eggs will not be laid all at once. Instead, the female will take periodic breathers from her task, and each time she moves away from the egg site the male will come to it and fertilize the eggs.

## CARING FOR THE EGGS

After all of the eggs have been laid and fertilized, the

parents normally will settle down to the job of tending them. This job consists primarily of hovering over the eggs, fanning them with their fins and occasionally mouthing them. The fanning keeps water moving over the eggs, thereby keeping them oxygenated and preventing sediment from settling on them; the mouthing keeps them clean and turns up bad eggs, which are destroyed.

Maintained at the same temperature at which the spawning took place, the eggs should hatch within a day and a half. The fry are comparatively large by aquarium fish standards but are nonetheless helpless, since they are still not able to swim; they adhere to the spot at which the eggs were hatched, wriggling away in a quivering clump. The parents attend them continuously. The fry at this stage require no food, as they still have attached to them the yolk sac, which nourishes them through their first few days of life. The yolk sac usually has been used up within four days of the time the fry have hatched, and at this point the fry become free-swimming. They are not good swimmers, making feeble darting motions rather than really swimming, but they at least are no longer confined to one well-defined spot in the tank and completely dependent on the parent fish for any movement that will be provided. They now need food, lots of it. If they get the right food, they'll grow quickly, becoming stronger and better able to take care of themselves every day; if they don't, they'll quickly die.

The previous rough chronology of events in the spawning tank assumes that the parents have been left with the eggs. It is not necessary to leave the parents with the eggs, because aeration can take the place of the fanning of the parents, and a good fungicide can take care of the mouthing. The decision to leave the parents or to remove the parents depends on what you value more, the spectacle of watching the parents care for their

*Aequidens rivulatus* (opposite, above) is commonly known as the green terror, and not without reason. It is a large predatory cichlid. However, like most other large cichlids, in a very large aquarium it usually will get along peaceably enough with one or more oscars. Photo by Ruth Brewer. Large swordplants (opposite, below) such as this *Echinodorus* species are among the few plants that can withstand the abuse of large digging cichlids such as oscars. They will stay rooted, however, only if they are well rooted before the oscars are placed into the tank. Photo by R. Zukal. A sand-bottomed rocky environment (above) makes an excellent habitat for oscars and other digging cichlids such as the African jewel cichlids, *Hemichromis bimaculatus,* shown here. Ounce for ounce, jewel cichlids are much more belligerent than oscars. Photo by Dr. D. Terver, Nancy Aquarium, France.

young or a guarantee that the eggs will not be eaten by the parents. For even though oscars generally are good parents, one or both of them might somewhere along the line eat the eggs ... or the fry. You never know when this might happen. Even pairs that have successfully tended flock after flock of youngsters occasionally indulge in a little infanticide; it's just a chance that you have to take if you want the full experience of breeding oscars. My personal opinion is that the rewards are well worth the gamble and that if you're lucky enough to get your pair to the point of laying eggs you ought, at least the first time, let them play out the role.

If you're bound and determined to get baby oscars, though, and never mind the sentimental garbage, do it this way: if the eggs have been laid on a rock or piece of slate, remove the egg-bearing object and place it into a non-toxic receptacle big enough to cover the eggs to a depth of six inches and to leave four or five inches of space around all sides of the rock. If the eggs are on a thin slab, prop something under one side so that the slab will be angled, with the higher end about two inches off the bottom. Place an airstone under the high end of the slab and set the aeration release rate so that a steady but not violent stream of air bubbles will play upward around the eggs. The bubble stream should go around, not onto, the eggs. The water in the hatching receptacle should be taken from the tank in which the parents spawned, and the water should have added to it a good strong solution of methylene blue, enough to turn the water dark blue. Acriflavine also can be used. Keep the temperature steady, and wait for the eggs to hatch. After they hatch, the fry will slowly tumble off the slate or whatever and fall to the bottom, where they'll wriggle around. Remove the slate when all of the fry have left it. When the fry have lost the yolk sac and actively seek food, feed them.

You should make up your mind about how you want to hatch the eggs, with the parents or without the parents, *before* you set up the spawning tank. If you are using a slate-bottom tank that contains gravel and you have decided to hatch the eggs without the parents, make sure you put in a suitable egg-site in the form of a rock or piece of slate. If the parents choose the site you've provided, and chances are good that they will, you'll be able to remove it, but if you don't provide a site or if they ignore your site and deposit the eggs right on the bottom of the tank, you won't be able to remove the eggs. If you're using an all-glass tank your chances of having the parents use the site you provide are better, because oscars don't often put the eggs directly onto a glass bottom. Resign yourself to the fact that the parents are not going to take kindly to the removal of their eggs; they'll attack the hand that removes them, and they'll be upset by their loss. If you do remove the eggs, separate the parents, because sometimes even the most harmonious pair will turn on one another if the eggs are taken from them.

## FEEDING THE FRY

Feeding the fry is the crucial point in the successful spawning and raising of aquarium fishes. In the raising of most species, the ability, or lack of ability, of the breeder to provide food that is both nourishing and small enough for the fry to ingest is the hinge on which success or failure swings. If he can provide the fry with good food, he's home free; if he can't, it's all over. Oscar breeders are fortunate in this respect, because baby oscars are easy to feed. They are large enough at the time they need food most to be able to eat newly hatched brine shrimp. They don't need the rotifiers and protozoans and one-celled algae that many other tropical fish fry need, and the job of the oscar breeder is thus made

*Cichlasoma nicaraguense* (above) reaches a size that makes it suitable as a tankmate for oscars. Photo by D. Tohie. The lip-tugging Jack Dempseys shown below are engaged in a prenuptial courtship ritual. This behavior is also sometimes carried out between two rival males who are each trying to establish territories. Oscars also engage in such behavior.

The intensity of the red coloration in red oscars varies from a pinkish gold color to a bright orange-red and is somewhat dependent upon the diet. Photo above by Dr. Herbert R. Axelrod. Photo below by Ken Lucas, Steinhart Aquarium.

easer. You can set up as many brine shrimp hatching containers as you need, and you can hatch as many brine shrimp as you need; the only thing it will cost you is money. When you consider the job they do for you, brine shrimp eggs are not expensive at all, really, and the little pink crustaceans that hatch from them will prove themselves invaluable to you in your task of getting the babies past their first few crucial weeks. You're going to lose some of the fry no matter how well you feed them, but without brine shrimp nauplii or some suitable substitute the losses would be 100%.

Collapsible brine shrimp hatchery units are available on the aquarium supplies market, but not many stores carry them, so most hobbyists who have a need for newly hatched brine shrimp use wide-mouth jars like gallon pickle or mayonnaise jars. The jars, filled halfway to two-thirds their capacity with the brine shrimp hatching solution, are tilted on their sides to provide maximum surface area. An airstone put into the jar will provide brisk agitation of the water, which will help the eggs to hatch. The eggs will hatch fairly quickly, according to the temperature and degree of salinity of the water. Follow the directions on the label of the container of eggs you purchase as to the amount of eggs you should use in each jar, salinity, and hatching temperature. Brine shrimp eggs vary in quality as to both percentage of hatch and the size of the nauplii; try different brands of eggs from different areas to see which work best for you.

Assuming that it would take you two days to obtain a good hatch of brine shrimp, the brine shrimp hatching unit should have been set up two days before the fry need them. Since you can't always determine with certainty exactly when the fry will have lost their yolk sacs, the best thing for you to do is to set up a minimum of two brine shrimp hatching units, with a day separating the initiation of each setup. The first unit should be set up the day after the fry hatch, and the second should be set up two days after the fry hatch. Therefore you should have food on hand two days from the time the fry hatch and a fresh supply three days after the fry hatch. Most of the shrimp can be kept alive for at least a few days after they've hatched, provided you continue to give them vigorous aeration, so the two hatching units set up under the schedule outlined above should provide the availability of a stock of food for the period of between two days and a week after the fry hatch. Depending on how many fry hatched and how many brine shrimp eggs were hatched, however, the stock of food provided by two jars might be nowhere near enough. The more jars you use and the greater the number of days over which you scatter the shrimp-hatching operation, the better are your chances of having an adequate supply of food when you need it. Since you already have a goodly investment in time, money and agonization in getting your oscars to spawn, it would be silly to stint in your efforts to provide the baby oscars with food. If you do stint, they'll die, so don't hold back on the pickle jars and shrimp eggs.

The best way to collect the shrimp nauplii from the hatching jars is to to turn off the aeration in the jar being harvested, turn the jar right-side up, focus a bright light at the midpoint in depth of the water in the jar, wait until the phototropic shrimp congregate at the light, and then siphon out the shrimp. Strain the siphon flow through a clean fine-meshed cloth, preferably white (a man's handkerchief is excellent), and dump the trapped shrimp into the tank holding the fry. You can rinse the shrimp in fresh water before you put them in with the oscar fry, thereby avoiding a build-up of salt in the tank, but it's not strictly necessary.

These young tiger oscars have not yet taken on their adult coloration. Photo by Dr. D. Terver, Nancy Aquarium, France.

This nicely marked juvenile oscar is completely at home in its sur-
roundings. Photo by A. Roth.

The tank shouldn't be too big (ten gallons is good, and even a five gallon tank will serve nicely), as you don't want to give the shrimp too much room to spread out; you want to make it easy for the fry to see and catch them. You can make things easier on the fry by putting a light near the bottom of their tank. Even though this light should be much less bright than the one you used to attract the shrimp in the hatching jar, the shrimp will still swim to it, and the fry will follow. You will be able to see the fry swallow the shrimp, and you'll be able to see how their bellies fill from a good feeding. It will be your job to see to it that those bellies stay as full as possible for as long as possible, because that's the best way to put growth on them.

As the babies grow you can test other foods on them to see whether they'll be able to take them. After the babies have reached a size at which they can take chopped tubifex worms, which should be only a matter of weeks, you can stop feeding the baby brine shrimp, except as an occasional treat. The young oscars will accept baby brine shrimp for a long time after they're not considered fry any more, and it will be a good food for them, but you'd have a tough time trying to hatch as many shrimp as they'd need for real growth after they reach the $\frac{3}{4}$-inch stage, so you have to make substitutions. As soon as they can accept frozen and dry foods, switch the fry over to these less expensive and more convenient items of diet. Probably the best growth producer for young oscars big enough to take them would be the fry of other fishes, but you'd have to have a very productive breeding program going for you to be able to supply enough fry to feed your baby oscars. Livebearer fry are best, because they have the greatest bulk at birth, but the fry of prolific egg-laying species like blue gouramis, if allowed to grow for a few weeks before being fed to the oscars, also can be valuable. The staple item of diet for your young oscars, once they're big enough to take them, should be whole tubifex worms, alternated with a good variety of meaty dried foods and frozen foods.

If they're placed on a successful feeding schedule and given enough room to grow, the baby oscars should reach a size of about $1\frac{1}{2}$ inches within three months, and when they do you'll have to start making arrangements for getting them out of your house and into someone else's. Determine how many of the youngsters you want to keep, if you want to keep any at all, and sell or give away the rest. Depending upon where you live and upon how successful other hobbyists in your area might have been in breeding oscars, you might have a very good market for your fish or you might have none at all. Even the most tropical fish conscious localities in the country, with the biggest metropolitan markets, have a limit to how many baby oscars can be absorbed at any given time, so don't think that you'll always have ready buyers for your oscars. You might, but you don't have any guarantee that you will. If you started out with only the two fish, the breeding pair, and have enough tank-space to house a number of babies and raise them to maturity, it would be a good idea to keep some and do exactly that, because you'll rarely have trouble in selling good-looking adult fish. But you'll have to resign yourself to a long wait before they're salable.

## NUMBER OF FRY RAISED

How many babies you'll have around to sell or trade or give away of course depends on how successful you are in avoiding the major mortality factors that carry off the greatest number of new *Astronotus,* but the parent oscars will cooperate with you in producing plenty of eggs for you to work with. The number of eggs produced by a given female at any spawning will

*Barbodes schwanenfeldi* (above), commonly known as the tinfoil barb because of its large silvery scales, reaches a length of 10 to 12 inches and is often chosen by hobbyists as a tankmate for oscars. The snakeskin gourami, *Trichogaster pectoralis* (below), at a 10-inch length is not as peaceful as some of the other members of the genus, and it is generally tough enough to get along with large cichlids in an aquarium. Photo by Dr. Herbert R. Axelrod.

This adult red oscar obviously has decided not to uproot the plants in its tank; some oscars will continually uproot plants, and some pay them no attention at all. Even the oscars that usually don't uproot plants, however, might take a different view of them during a spawning period. Photo by A. Roth.

vary according to the age of the fish and her over-all health, but even the youngest and most marginally conditioned spawning female will produce a minimum of 300 eggs, and older females in good condition can produce thousands at each spawning. On a basis of 100% fertilization, that leaves plenty of room for infant oscar mortality and still leaves many babies to raise. As mentioned before, many babies will die on first-time breeders no matter how much effort is expended in taking care of the spawn, so don't feel badly if out of 500 eggs or so you're left with only 25 babies that you're able to grow to salable size. A 20-1 egg-to-juvenile ratio would hardly satisfy a professional breeder or experienced amateur breeder, but for a newcomer to the scanty ranks of oscar breeders it wouldn't be anything to be too ashamed of, especially since the ratio should become much more respectable as experience is gained.

# 6.

# DISEASES OF OSCARS

With the exception of treating for one specific ailment, ichthyophthiriasis, I think that the best thing to do with the main run of aquarium fishes when they get sick is to destroy them. It's more humane than making them linger while barraging them with a slew of chemicals designed to get rid of their parasites or cure their diseases, and it's safer in the long run. Oscars, however, are not included in the definition of the main run of aquarium fishes, at least not by owners who have had them around for a while and have grown attached to them, so let's cover some of the common disorders that affect oscars. We can't cover them all, but there's no need to, because there are many excellent books devoted completely to covering the recognition and treatment of disease of tropical aquarium fishes. Specifically recommended is *Diseases of Aquarium Fishes*, by Dr. Robert J. Goldstein.

Oscars are less susceptible to some fish ailments than other aquarium fishes and more susceptible to others. In the case of those ailments to which they are more susceptible, the heightened susceptibility usually is the result of the oscar's size or pugnacious nature. The growth of the fungus *Saprolegnia* on untreated wounds caused by fighting is an example. Small, comparatively peaceful schooling fishes such as neons and zebra danios suffer from fungus invasions much less frequently than oscars, mostly because they are much less likely to

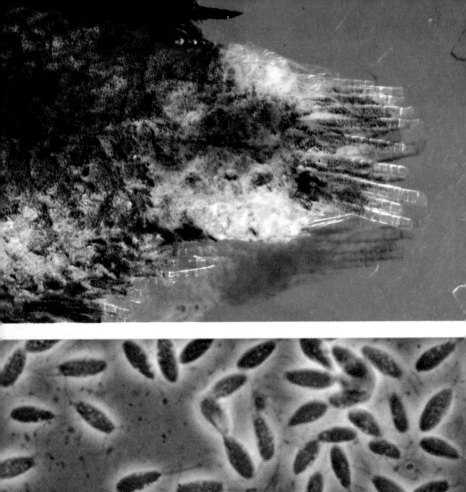

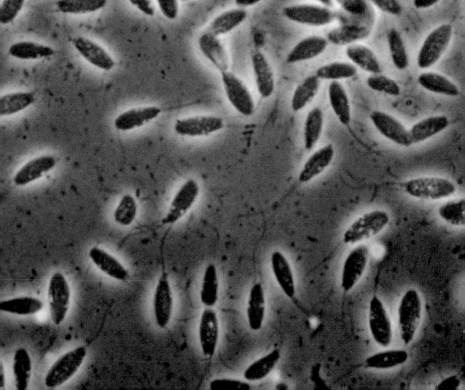

Bacterial and fungal infections can destroy fin tissue (opposite, top) unless treated promptly. *Hexamita*, a flagellated protozoan (opposite, bottom), is thought by fish pathologists to be the primary cause of hole-in-the-head disease. Also called hexamitiasis, the disease is reported quite frequently in oscars and other large cichlids. It can be treated by giving the fish internal doses of Flagyl® (usually in the food). Photo by Frickhinger. The photos on this page show lesions caused by hole-in-the-head disease in discus. Upper photo by Frickhinger. Lower photo by Dr. H. Reichenbach-Klinke.

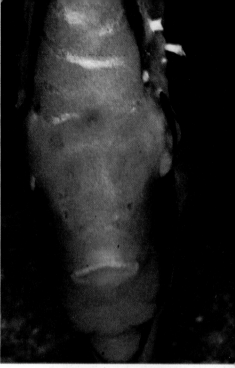

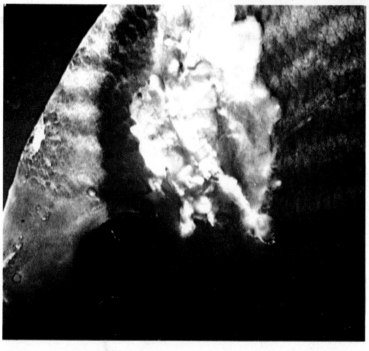

sustain wounds when maintained with their own kind, yet oscars are much less frequently infested with the dinoflagellate *Oodinium* than bettas and killies, probably because one of the greatest single contributors to the outbreak of velvet disease (as *Oodinium* infections are generally called) is the buildup of unsanitary conditions in the small tanks in which bettas and many killies generally are kept.

The most common ailment of aquarium fishes is ichthyophthiriasis, commonly if not affectionately known as ich or ick. This disease, caused by a protozoan parasite of the genus *Ichthyophthirius,* causes the outbreak of a rash of tiny white specks all over the body and fins of the affected fish. The white spots are not the disease organism itself but are cysts in which the protozoans live prior to adopting a free-swimming phase and actively seeking a host fish. There are two good things about ich: it's not a quick killer, being more of an irritant to the fish, and it's easy to cure. Ich infestations usually, but not always, are caused by subjecting the fish to abrupt drop in temperature or by exposing it to contact with ich-infested fish without any drop in temperature. Ich is highly transmissible; if one fish in a tank has ich, others in the tank usually soon will be infested, too. The best way to cure ich is to ask your pet dealer for the best ich remedy he carries and then use that remedy according to the manufacturer's directions. There are a number of excellent products that will soon clear a tank of ich.

Velvet is more stubborn and difficult to cure, but you can buy good anti-velvet specifics, too. Oodinium infections evidence themselves by the appearance of tiny yellowish-red granules over the body of the affected fish; they give the skin a velvety appearance. The best way to avoid velvet is to keep the tank clean.

Although it can't be classed as a disease or put down

to infestation by parasites, indigestion happens to be something that oscars are occasionally troubled with, and usually for the same reason people are: overeating. Oscars are gluttons and will keep on eating as long as you keep on providing the food; again like people, they don't always get away with it. An oscar with indigestion shows his indisposition by sulking and refusing to eat; a fish so affected also sometimes shows peculiar body orientation in the water, standing still or swimming with its head down. The latter movement often is accompanied by a slight cant to the body so that the fish is not perfectly vertical in the water. Sometimes an oscar with indigestion will do barrel-rolls throughout the tank, and sometimes it will even give out with a good approximation of a human burp. The best cure for indigestion is to leave the fish without food for as long as it shows any distress and, when it is fed again, to offer only small foods, preferably alive. Keep the tank dimly lighted or completely dark during the period that food is kept withdrawn, and don't do anything to startle the fish. Some oscar owners treat their bellyache-ridden fish by adding a few pinches of epsom salts to the water, but this shouldn't be necessary.

The best way to keep oscars healthy is to avoid excesses in all forms, whether in temperature range, amount and type of food offered, or water quality. Don't chill or overheat the fish, don't overfeed the fish, don't subject the fish to contamination by exposing it to a sick fish, don't crowd the fish, don't let pollutants build up in their tanks, and you should have very few disease problems on your hands. Treat oscars well and they'll reward you with years and years of entertainment and fascination and even a fishy sort of reciprocal affection ... and perhaps also a few thousand baby oscars; treat them badly and they'll give you only the kind of grief you give them.

# OSCARS